Adventures of the Clumsy Ninja

Zac Tyler

Chapter 1

Tony was not sure how he was going to explain this to the store clerk. It was his second costume in two weeks and if it had been near Halloween, he might have been able to spin a tale; in the middle of February, not so much.

He hesitantly opened the door of the shop and a bell chimed, notifying the shopkeeper of his arrival. It was Mrs. Dunaway. Tony groaned internally. *Why couldn't it have been Mr. Dunaway?*

"Anthony!" cried Mrs. Dunaway, peering over her glasses perched on the edge of her nose; a little twitch, a tiny sniff, and they would fall off.

"Hi, Mrs. Dunaway," Tony said, trying to reciprocate her enthusiasm.

"How's your mother, eh? And your

father?"

She always asked both the questions together without waiting for an answer.

"Fine," he said, briefly, trying, unsuccessfully, to move away towards the "action star" costumes.

"Where are your manners, Anthony? Answer properly."

Tony, who had already turned, closed his eyes for a moment and shook his head infinitesimally. *Always.*

"My parents are fine, thank you, Mrs. Dunaway. I am fine, too. How are you and Mr. Dunaway?" he said, trying hard to keep the exasperation and false sweetness out of his voice. *She is just trying to be nice.*

"Now that's a good boy. You are almost twelve now. Soon you will be a teenager; plenty of time to misbehave then." She said, giving him a small wink and shadow of a smile over her glasses.

Tony just smiled and before he could be drawn into another conversation about his behavior, moved quickly to the costumes in the back. He made a good show of trying to mull over all the options. S

ince it was off season, he was not surprised to see all the bestsellers well in stock: Batman, Spider-Man, Captain America, and Iron Man. But after hovering what, in his mind, was an acceptable amount of time, he moved to the one he desired. A steely black costume, complete with the mask and those flat-lined shoes: A ninja.

"Hey, Mrs. Dunaway, I want this in my size." He called over to the old woman who was hitting her calculator on the counter very hard.

"The machines these days; can't get them working," she muttered as she made her way to the only customer in the shop.

"What, this? Again? Didn't you get this last week?" She said, looking at the costume Tony was pointing to.

"Well, yeah."

"So? What do you need another one for? You preparing for the wrong day, Anthony. Get some flowers. Got yourself a special someone?"

Tony decided to go with the truth, dumb as it may sound, while disregarding the comment about

Valentine's day.

"I tore the first one." He said quickly, hoping she would not ask anything else.

He was wrong.

"Tore it? How come?"

Again, he went with the truth.

"Well, I put it on and before I had

moved five feet, it caught on one of the nails that were sticking out from my bed and now it is almost in two pieces."

Mrs. Dunaway didn't say anything for a good ten seconds. Then she walked away towards the back of the shop, apparently to get Tony's size costume. Tony heard the tail end of her muttering.

"....dumbest thing I've ever heard, I tell ya."

Chapter 2

"Hey, Pa, what's so special about Valentine's Day?" Tony thought he would not think about his trip to Mrs. Dunaway's this afternoon but he couldn't help but wonder.

Tony's father was perched on his armchair, one he occupied daily at 9:00 pm without fail, always with a newspaper opened to the crossword.

He didn't glance away from the paper.

"Huh? What day?"

"V-A-L-E-N-T-I-N-E-S", Tony articulated.

"Oh, that. Why didn't you say so earlier?" he looked up from his crossword, a rarity. "It is a day invented by TV people so that women can get expensive stuff from their husbands."

"Really? Is that what you think?" a voice came floating from the other room. The alarm on Tony's dad's face said it all.

"I mean, it is nothing short of sacred, obviously," he said sheepishly, trying to do some damage control as his wife came in from the other room.

"Well, the teacher was way off," said Tony.

"What did the teacher say?" asked

Tony's mother, as his father looked as if he wouldn't open his mouth anytime soon.

"Mrs. Rigby said that Valentine 's Day is for loved ones. A whole day just for love."

"Hmm. Is that correct, Michael?" Tony's mother directed the question to his father, giving him a look that conveyed the answer all too clearly.

"Yes, that old thing. Love." He said

and again absorbed himself in the crossword.

"Twenty-six across...five letters... *Japanese cloak-and-dagger fighter...*"

Chapter 3

Tony couldn't get Valentine's Day out of his head the next day as he walked in the corridor. *A whole day for love.* His mother had told him how people gave cards and flowers to their loved ones to show their affection. *Wouldn't it be nice to give Emma flowers?*

Bearing this thought in mind, he had

plucked a few flowers from the school ground and put them in his bag. Now he was contemplating if he should give them to Emma or not.

Emma was the girl who sat two seats diagonally left to him. He didn't know why but he found her very sweet and hers was the first face that prompted in his mind when he learnt the significance of Valentine's Day.

He was immersed in these thoughts when he spotted Emma among the throng of students scattered in the corridor, during the break between classes. He made an impulse decision.

He was going to give the flowers to her. *But here?! In front of everyone?* Again doubt entered his mind. He was still in a quandary when he didn't notice and tripped over something and fell face down on the floor.

A shot of laughter rose up in the corridor. Tony turned around instinctively to see what had caused him to trip. What he saw made his blood boil: leering and sticking out his foot was Toby Duhamel. *Toby*.

He was an eighth grader who had had an axe to grind with Tony ever since Tony beat him in a game of ping pong.

"Oops," he sneered. "Maybe you'll watch where you are going next time."

Tony got up angrily, red in the face. His eyes instinctively looked for

Emma. She wasn't there. *Good, maybe she didn't see that. That jerk, Toby.*

He made his way to the washroom to clean off the dust and wash his hands. *I would get back at him, someday.* He was thinking furiously. It was five minutes to the class. He felt he should go while he's there.

He had consecutive classes up next. He entered the urinal and locked the door, his mind still reeling from Toby's sneer.

He was about done when he heard the bathroom door open and several pair of feet scampered in. He recognized one of the voices.

"We'll do it tomorrow, okay? After school." Toby was saying in a low voice.

"What about the intruder alarm? What if we get caught?" a panicked voice, belonging to John Daniels, one of Toby's gang said.

"You're *not* gonna chicken out on me now, John! And I told you: the alarm doesn't work. The last time it got broken, nobody bothered to fix it."

Tony was holding his breath. Whatever they were planning was not good, otherwise they wouldn't have needed to do their talking in hushed voices in a toilet. He was barely letting air out lest they should feel his presence.

"Ok," Toby said with finality. "Tomorrow it is."

And they left the washroom. Tony let out a sigh. Only one place in the school had its alarm broken. This Valentine's was going to be Halloween for Tony.

Chapter 4

Tony did not know what the endgame of Toby and his cronies was but he was willing to bet that it wasn't anything noble. Plus his current anger over Toby had made him doubly willing to go through with it.

He had the ninja costume in his school bag, a slightly bulking sight. All day whenever he could find time, he would try to look for Toby or John as he didn't know who the third person was. But once or twice when he did find them, they were not doing anything out of the ordinary.

So he focused all energies on the second most important task of the day: how to give flowers to Emma? He had thought out a game plan.

As the teacher ploughed on about volumes of irregular figures, Tony was stealing glances at Emma. *It was Valentine's Day. He had to do something today*. He had seen boys give girls flowers in the corridors in between classes and even the other way around.

He was surprised that Emma had not received one yet. *Pleasantly surprised*. His notebook was open in front of him and the pen was poised in a writing position, the nib merely an inch away from the page.

"Anthony!" said Mr. Lithgow.

Tony jerked back to attention and in doing so the pen touched the paper and drew a long blue line from top to the end. Mr. Lithgow sighed.

"Anthony, I know a daydreamer when I see one."

"Sorry, Mr. Lithgow. Won't happen again." He said as he flipped on to the next page.

"Better not," the teacher said sternly.

Tony drew a long breath. *Maybe not today.*

Tony was desperately trying to get into the ninja costume but he had only able to entangle himself more. *Couldn't I have tried it at home at least once!*

His one leg was inside and the other one was nowhere to be found. It was getting dark. He was hiding behind the library. There was fat chance someone would walk into him there as it was already past school time and the guards didn't usually make their rounds till late in the evening. This was the ideal time to get changed.

But fate, and his usual clumsiness, had other things in mind as he tried desperately to get the other foot in the tangled legs of the costume. Before he could break through, he lost his balance and fell down.

It was a humbling moment, he thought. *Better be quick before Toby sees me like this. He won't even need to stick out his foot this time.*

Chapter 5

He got dressed finally and put his school clothes in the bag and hid it in the bushes behind the library.

From his vantage point, he had a clear view to the indoor entrance of the library. It was empty and all the lights were off, except the one in the hallway.

The light from the hallway crossed the glass door of the library in a haze. Toby was holding the mask in his hand. It was getting darker by the minute and still there was no sign of Toby.

More than once the thought crossed his mind that it was not worth it, that maybe it was something harmless that Toby was up to.

But whenever this thought crossed his mind, he would also remember the urgency in Toby's voice and the fear in John's. *No, it is something terrible.*

Just as he was thinking this, he heard some voices coming from the front of the library. He hastily put on the mask and peered around from behind the wall of the library.

All he could see was darkness from one eye and limited visibility from the other one. In his haste, he had put on the mask wrongly. *Good thing the bad guys didn't see me this way.* He corrected the mask and enjoyed the full view.

Two boys were making their way to the library, flashlights in hand, talking in hushed whispers, which owing to the immense quiet could be heard from afar. Tony could make out the silhouette of the boy in front. *Toby*.

He didn't know where their third partner was. Maybe he was mistaken. Maybe it was only John and Toby.

Toby was working on the door of the library while John held a lookout. Tony slowly emerged from behind the wall and slowly started walking towards the main door to get a better look.

Before he had covered a significant distance, his foot got stuck in bushes and he fell with a thud. *Oh, shoot, please don't let them hear that.*

He didn't get up immediately because the noise from the front had stopped abruptly. *They had heard it.* Panic rose in Tony's chest like gas getting filled in a balloon. His heart was thumping madly.

What would happen if they saw him? Would they beat him? He decided if they caught him, he would scream as loud as he could to get the attention of the guards.

"You heard that?" Toby's voice asked in a low tone.

"Y-yes. What do you think it is? A

guard?" John's shaky voice reached Tony's head. *Good, I am not the only one afraid.*

"Go check it out," Toby said.

Maybe he is too scared to check it out himself.

"Why me? You go check it out," John was probably thinking the same thing.

Toby didn't say anything but rather

peered around from the front of the library. It was dark and Tony was in a black costume lying on the grass.

Toby couldn't spot anything. He hesitantly started walking along the wall when quick footsteps from behind made him turn.

"Hey, it's done. The guards are way around the other end of the school. We have probably got fifteen, twenty minutes at the max." The third person had come back. *So they have created a diversion. Calling the guards was out of question.*

"Good, good," Toby said distractedly, still looking for the source of the noise. But the urgency of the matter made him turn back.

Tony breathed a sigh of relief and his heartbeat started to normalize. *Shadows are a Ninja's best weapon.* He got up and making sure he did not fall again, he slowly walked towards the front.

Toby had managed to open the front door and just as he had said yesterday, the alarm did not go off.

"John, keep a lookout. I and Billy will get the books." Toby ordered and he moved quickly inside, leaving John outside alone.

"Ok, Toby, no problem. I will keep the lookout. That's what I am good for," John grumbled under his breath.

Toby and the third person, Billy, had

entered the library and were putting the books in a large sack. Tony could see from a window on the side wall, they were collecting first editions and rare books.

He realized what they were doing: they were stealing books to sell on the black market. *I have to stop them.* With the guards gone, it fell upon Tony to stop these three or otherwise a significant portion of the books from the library will be gone.

But there was a catch: there were

three of them and one of him. They were significantly stronger than him. He couldn't overpower them. He could go and find the guards but by then they would have easily escaped.

Tony could see John haphazardly moving the flash light here and there, never keeping it in one place for more than a few seconds. Suddenly, he had a spark of inspiration. *Eureka.*

But for that, he needed to get rid of John. He glanced inside the library and saw that Toby and Billy were right at the back of the library, still pouring books in the sack.

Chapter 6

Tony was running out of time. He picked up a stone and threw it a few feet away from John. In the dark he couldn't see anything and when the stone landed, the thud made him jump and give a little yelp.

"Hey, what's wrong?" Toby hushed in a furious whisper that carried all the way to the front.

"Somebody is here. They threw a stone at me." John's voice was filled with panic.

"Don't be stupid, Jack. There's nobody there," Billy had moved closer to the entrance to talk to John. "We are almost done. Just hold the fort, alright."

Billy went back to the back and Tony again threw a stone, this time closer to John.

He jumped atleast a foot in the air and flung the torch in the direction from where the stone came from. Tony jumped just in time to avoid the light.

"W-Who's there?" John said, in a slightly high pitched voice.

He started walking tentatively towards the place where Tony was hiding. Tony drew back further, closer to the wall, in the bushes. His black costume made him virtually invisible.

John went straight past Tony's hiding position. Tony had to move quickly. He ran on soft feet behind John, in the opposite direction towards the entrance of the library.

Before John could turn, he had made his way to the inside of the library entrance and into the dark.

Toby and Billy were nowhere to be seen but Tony could see the light from their torches flickering in one of the last rows.

John was making his way back and apparently satisfied that there was nobody throwing stones at him, took his spot in front of the library door, with his back to the entrance.

Now, all Tony had to do was to find the position behind the desk of the librarian. He knew it was there because he had seen it, but it was very difficult to navigate his way in the dark.

He was crawling towards the desk and once safely behind it he started feeling for the glass of the fire alarm. *Come on, come on. We're so close.*

After about half of minute of his hands searching the wall behind the desk like a spider, he found the switch. He immediately broke the glass and a loud ring erupted.

The ring was such that if someone was in the other corner of the school, they could still hear the bell. It was designed for such purpose. The ringing was deafening. He could see the lights from torches moving in a zig-zag manner.

He had managed to baffle the intruders. It would take the guards less than three minutes to come to the library from any point in the school.

Now all Tony needed to do was to escape from the library. He could hear running footsteps and it seemed that Toby and Billy were running as fast as they could towards the entrance.

"John!! What the hell is going on?!"
Toby shouted over the ringing of the
alarm.

"I've no clue!" shouted Jack, still
standing perplexed at the entrance,
his torch pointed downwards,
mesmerized by the event unfolding in
front of him.

"You said the *alarm* didn't work!"
shouted Billy, in a clearly accusatory
tone, as he ran towards the entrance,
a few steps behind Toby.

"The intruder alarm, *genius!* The fire alarm clearly works." Toby growled.

Just as they crossed the main desk behind which Tony was hiding, he crept outside and he could see many lights at the entrance. *The guards were here!*

A huge sense of relief washed over Tony as he knew that he had managed to thwart *Toby*. He triumphantly got up and started walking briskly towards the entrance and in his haste and limited visibility hit on a shelf. And then there was blackness.

"Hey, kid, wake up." Someone was shaking him. He felt a few drops of cold water on his face.

"I'm up. I'm okay." Tony said groggily. He opened his eyes and his vision sharpened. The guard Jimmy was cradling his head. His ninja mask was off.

"You sounded the alarm?"

"Yeah....yeah," replied Tony, still not fully cognizant.

There was a momentary silence.

"You are a brave kid."

"Or stupid."

"Often times, it is difficult to differentiate between the two, I agree," said Jimmy with a chuckle.

"Where are the intruders, you got them?"

"Yeah, yeah," Jimmy said, offhandedly, as if Tony shouldn't concern himself with such matters. "They are in the security officer's room. We are contacting Principal Clayton right now. She will inform their parents."

Tony nodded. He didn't know what else to say. Then he saw the mask.

"I would appreciate..." he started but Jimmy cut him off.

"Yeah, yeah. Don't worry. I just want the good old days to come back when kids gave flowers to each other on Valentine's day." He sighed. "Now everybody wants to be Batman. By the way, how did you lose consciousness?"

Tony pressed his memory.

"Well I was running towards the

entrance as I saw your lights and I hit a shelf and that's the last thing I remember." He said sheepishly.

Another silence.

"You are one clumsy ninja, kid," chuckled Jimmy.

Made in the USA
San Bernardino, CA
22 November 2017